# WHAT ARE MAGNETS?

## A CHILD'S GUIDE TO UNDERSTANDING MAGNETS

### SCIENCE BOOK FOR ELEMENTARY SCHOOL CHILDREN'S HOW THINGS WORK BOOKS

AF442201

Speedy Publishing LLC

40 E. Main St. #1156

Newark, DE 19711

www.speedypublishing.com

Copyright 2017

All Rights reserved. No part of this book may be reproduced or used in any way or form or by any means whether electronic or mechanical, this means that you cannot record or photocopy any material ideas or tips that are provided in this book.

In this book, we're going to talk about magnets and magnetic fields. So, let's get right to it!

# WHAT IS A MAGNET?

All matter in the universe is made up of very tiny particles that we can't see. These "building blocks" of matter are called atoms. Atoms are made up of:

- Protons, which have a charge that's positive

- Electrons, which have a charge that's negative

- Neutrons, which have no charge

CERAMIC MAGNET

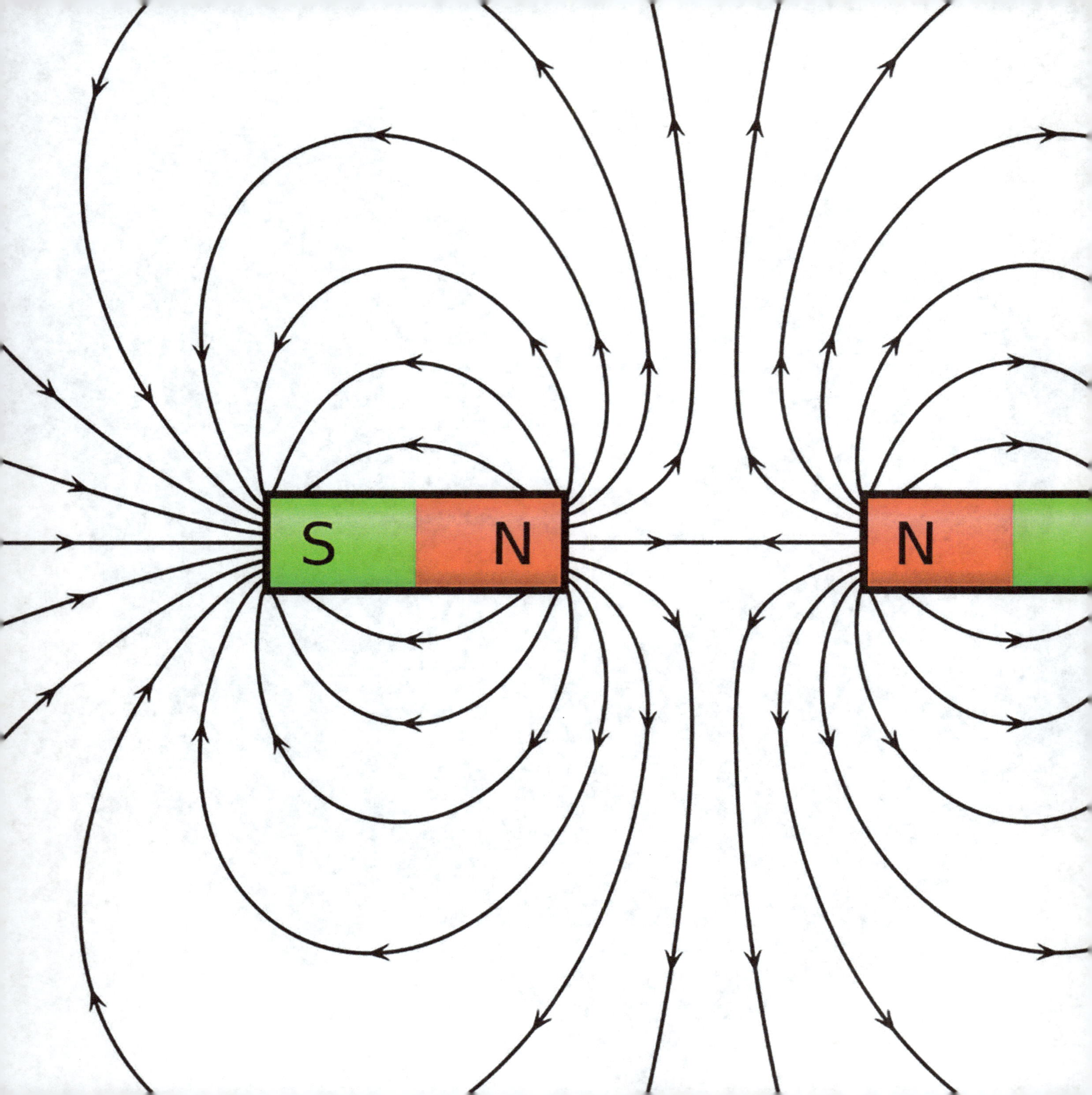

S
N
N

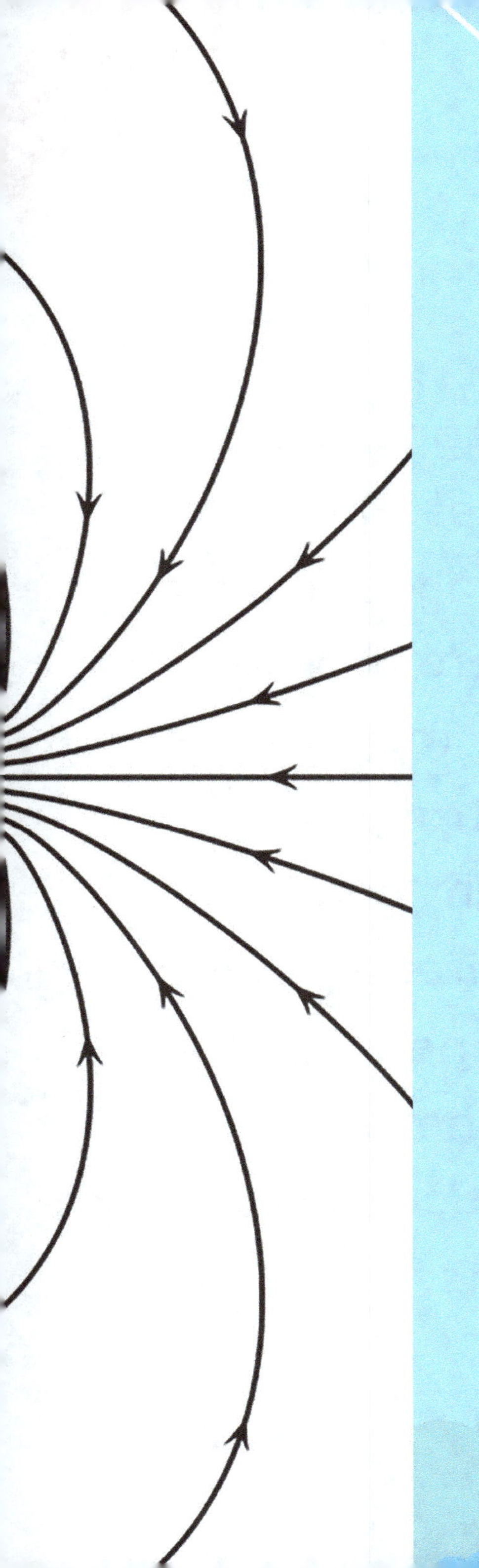

ost of the time, the electrons in an atom just spin around its core in random directions. However, when the electrons all revolve in the same direction, they create a force. This force, which we can't see with our eyes, is called a "magnetic force." All permanent magnets have this magnetic force. Another way to describe this force is to say that it's created by moving electrons, which are basically currents of electricity.

You may have played with a magnet before. Magnets come in different shapes. They have two poles. The poles are where the magnetic force of the magnet is the strongest. There is a north pole as well as a south pole to every magnet. On a horseshoe-shaped magnet, one straight end is the north pole and the other straight end is the south. If you have a nail made of iron and you hold it closer and closer to the magnet, you can actually feel the pull that the magnet has as it attracts the iron nail. Magnets exert control over objects before they touch the objects.

punch me
in
the
face

# AN EXPERIMENT TO SEE HOW A MAGNETIC FIELD LOOKS

If you get a parent or teacher to help you, you can see a sample of how an invisible magnetic field works. To see the magnetic field in action, you will need a small magnet, some iron filings, and a sheet of paper. Place the magnet on a table, then place the sheet of paper on top of it. Carefully spread the iron filings on top of the paper. You will see a pattern emerge. This pattern shows you the force of the magnetic field.

# ANCIENT PEOPLE KNEW ABOUT MAGNETS

Just because you know that something works, you may or may not understand why it works. Ancient people knew about the magnetic properties of stones for thousands of years, but they didn't fully understand why or how those properties worked. They thought the power of magnetic stones was a form of magic.

ANCIENT CHINESE MAGNETIC COMPASS

LODESTONE

The ancient Greeks as well as the ancient Romans were aware that a certain type of stone that was eventually called a lodestone could attract iron pieces to itself. Lodestones are made of a material called magnetite and other minerals. However, most natural magnetite doesn't form into lodestones that have magnetic power. Scientists believe that the powerful magnetic fields that accompany lightning bolts give this special form of magnetite its magnetic quality.

The origin of the word "lodestone" means "course" and "stone." Ancient peoples soon discovered that if they had a piece of lodestone and they suspended it in mid-air, it would point to the north. This method was used for navigation and eventually became the basis for how the compass was developed.

LODESTONE

FENG SUI COMPASS

The ancient Greeks and Romans weren't the only ones who understood how to use the magnetic properties of lodestones. The ancient Chinese used to have detailed wooden pieces that held lodestones. These compasses were used to arrange the objects in a room through the practice of an art called "Feng Shui." Many people still use "Feng Shui" when they do the interior design for their houses.

Even though ancient people used stones that had natural magnetism, it wasn't until scientists understood atomic structure that magnets were truly understood.

The science behind the connection between atomic structure and magnetic fields was only discovered over the last one hundred fifty years.

HORSESHOE MAGNET

# SOME IMPORTANT THINGS TO KNOW ABOUT MAGNETS

Each magnet has a north-seeking pole and a south-seeking pole.

If you place two magnets close to each other and arrange their north poles facing each other, they will repel or force each other apart. If you place two magnets close to each other and arrange their south poles facing each other, they will repel or force each other apart.

If you place a north pole of one magnet close to the south pole of a second magnet, they will attract and eventually snap together as you move them closer and closer. In other words, unlike poles will attract each other and like poles will repel each other.

All magnets create fields around them that influence other objects that are magnetic. These fields are called magnetic fields.

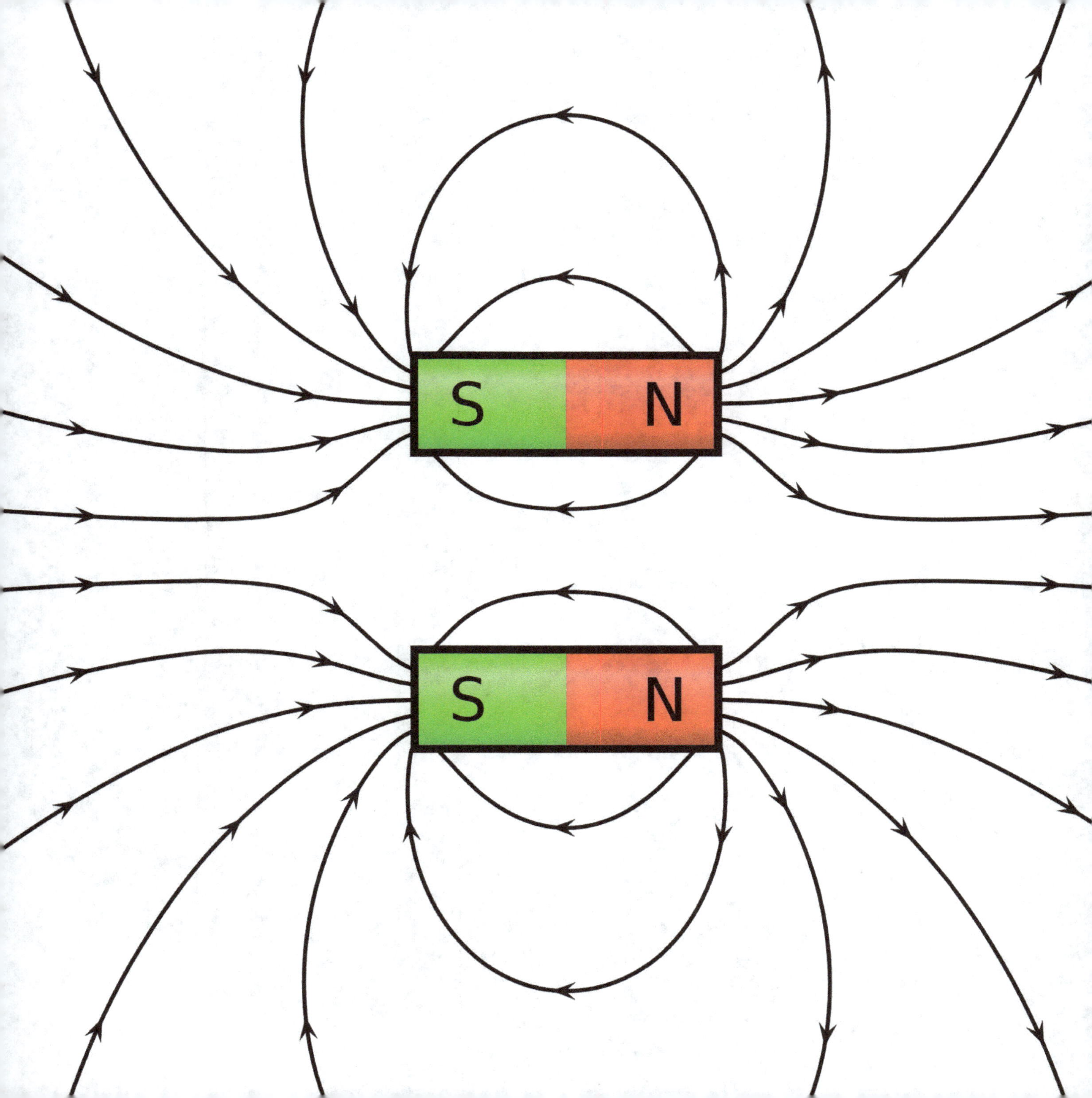

S
N
S
N

330
0
30
60
N
NW
NE
E
SW
SE
S
JAPAN

A compass works because its magnetic piece points roughly to the north pole of the Earth. If you take a magnet and cut it in half, you will get a surprising result. Each piece will become its own magnet with a north as well as a south pole.

Magnetic fields can penetrate air but they can also penetrate other types of materials. When you put a piece of paper on your refrigerator door using a magnet, the magnetic force is able to penetrate the paper.

A FIELD INDICATOR IS USED TO ENSURE
THE BRAKE PADS

f you take a magnet and rub it against an iron nail, you can transform that nail so that it has magnetic properties too. This process is called "magnetization."

BAR MAGNET

# WHERE DO WE GET MAGNETS?

There are only a few types of elements that have the correct atomic structure that allows electrons to create a current. Both iron and steel, which is composed primarily of iron, can be used to make magnets.

# THE EARTH IS A GIANT MAGNET

E ven though ancient peoples used compasses, they really didn't know the reason why a compass points north. The first scientist to explain why compasses work the way they do was an English scientist by the name of William Gilbert.

PLANET EARTH

WILLIAM GILBERT

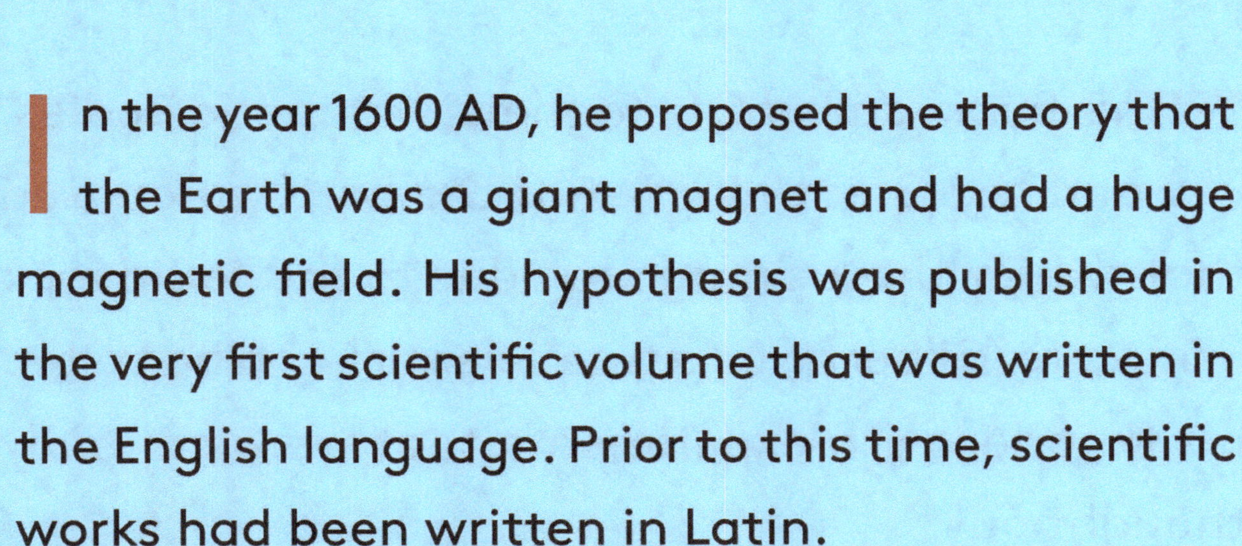

In the year 1600 AD, he proposed the theory that the Earth was a giant magnet and had a huge magnetic field. His hypothesis was published in the very first scientific volume that was written in the English language. Prior to this time, scientific works had been written in Latin.

This book, called Of Magnets, Magnetic Bodies, and the Great Magnet of the Earth, proposed that the Earth was magnetic due to the liquid rock in its core. Gilbert was a true scientist and he tested his theories with experiments that were carefully thought out.

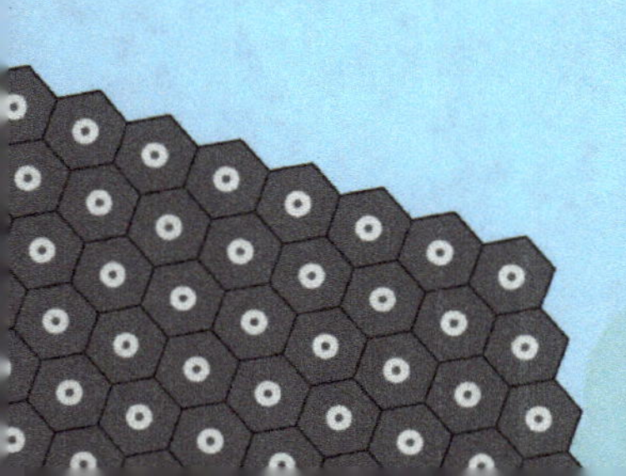

LIBYEN
ÄGYPTEN
SAUDI-
ARABIEN
Nedjed
IRAK
TÜRKEI
KASACHSTAN
AFGHANISTAN
OMAN
INDIEN
QATAR
ARABISCHES
RUB AL KHALI
CHARKOW
ALEXANDRIA
ANKARA

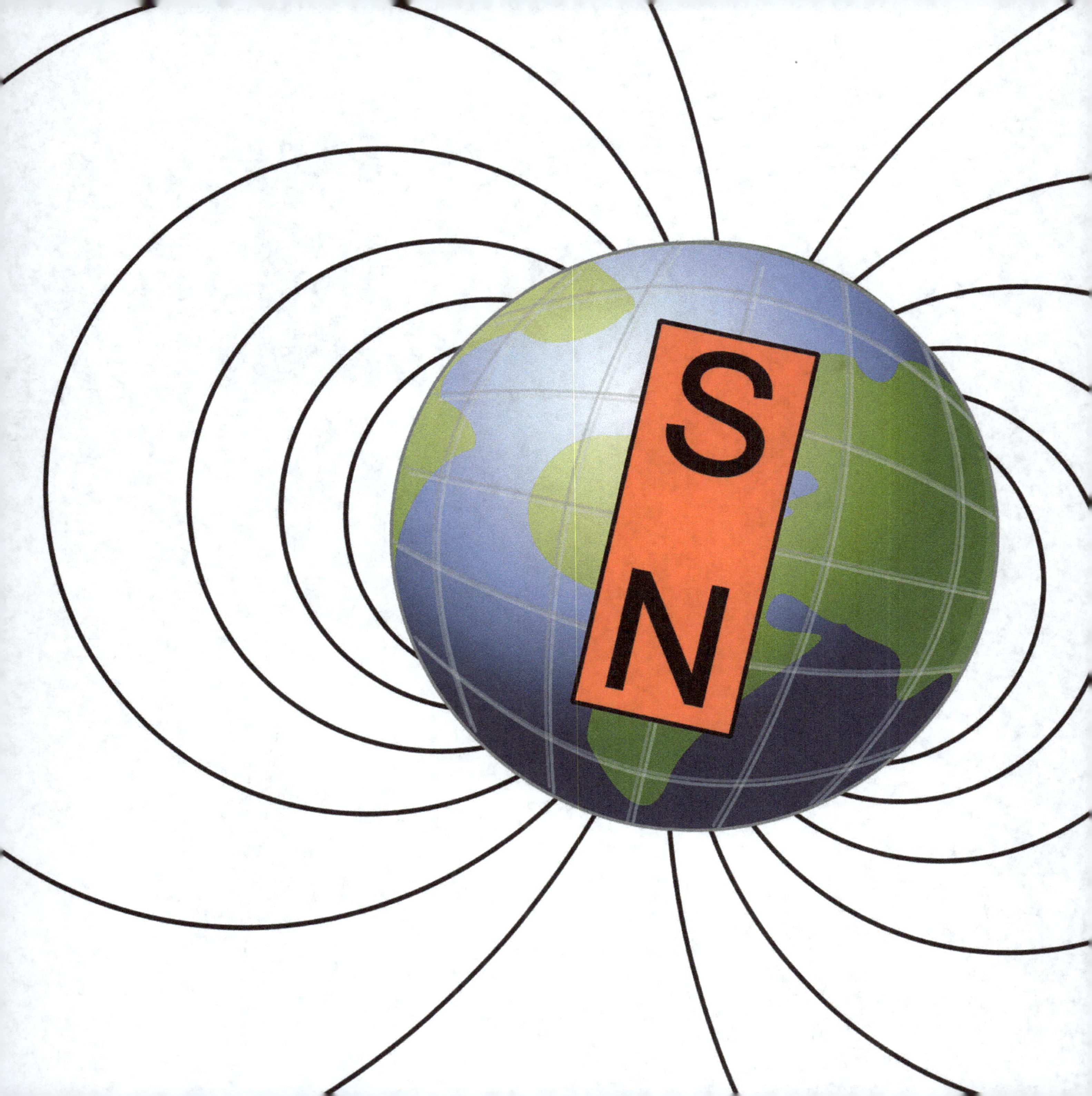
S
N

Gilbert's theories were correct. The Earth's core is composed of magnetic rocks such as iron. As the Earth spins, the iron in its core also spins creating a magnet. Earth's north pole and south pole are its magnetic poles. The Earth is a giant magnet floating in space.

Earth's magnetic field expands into space and creates a region called the magnetosphere. This magnetic field helps to protect us from the dangerous radiation that bombards us from the Sun called the solar wind. Around the poles, the magnetosphere is shaped similar to a funnel so the solar wind interacts with our atmosphere. When this occurs, the interaction creates the beautiful aurora borealis, also called the Northern Lights.

Humans are the not the only ones who use a compass. Birds and sea creatures use the Earth's magnetic field to navigate around the world. They are able to sense the magnetosphere, which helps them to fly or swim in specific directions.

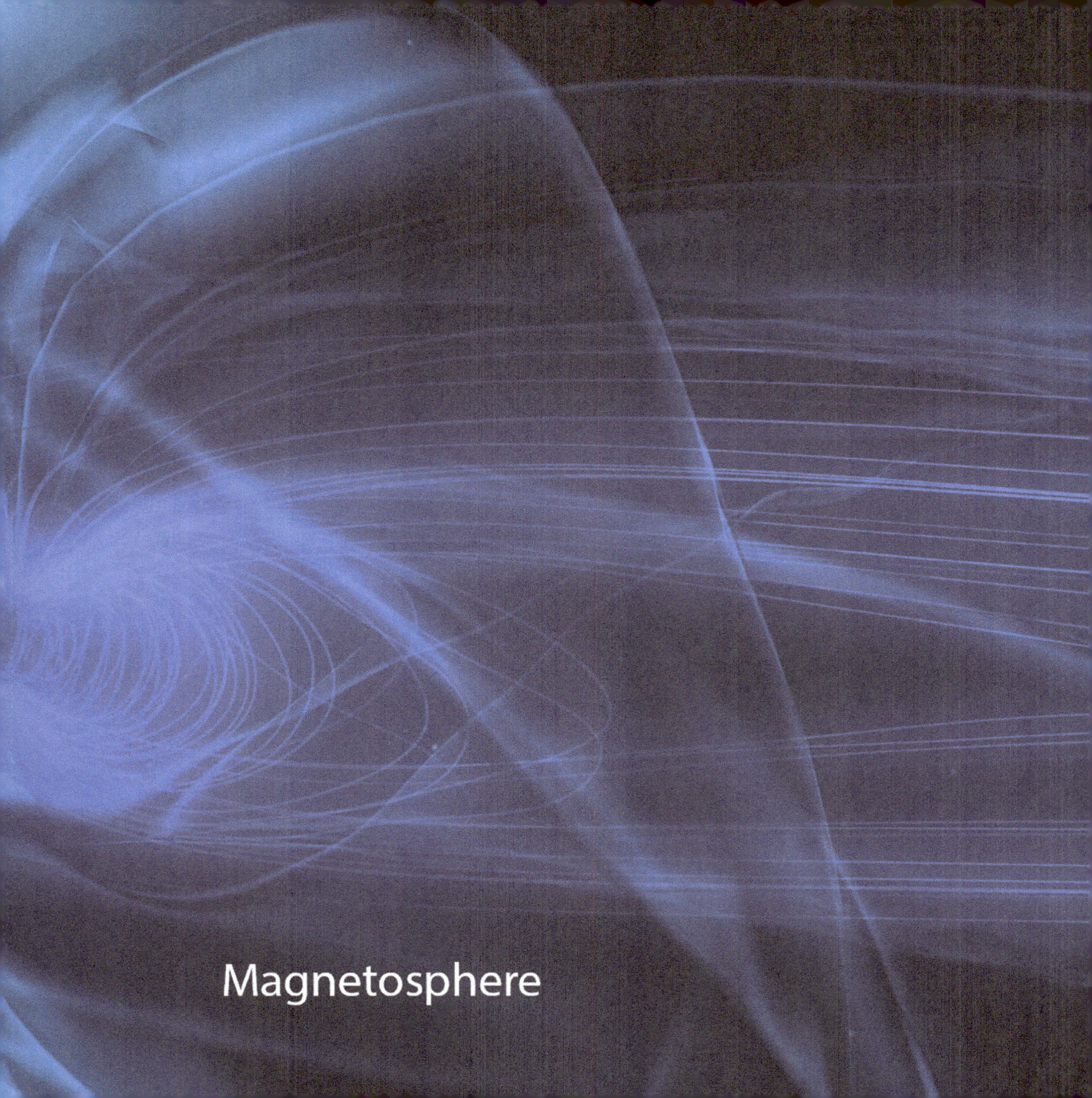

Magnetosphere

If the Earth wasn't a magnet, a compass that you held would point to the nearest magnetic material if there was some around. This actually happens in places on Earth where the surface has a great deal of magnetic material. It throws off the normal workings of a compass.

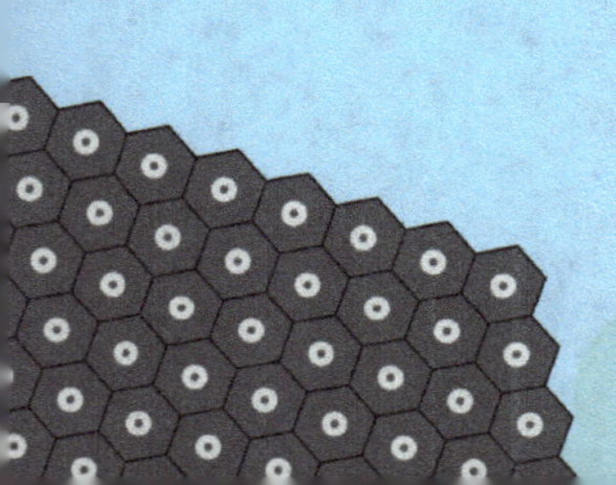

Cosmos
Lawlers MgCO3
Glory Bore V Fe
Forrest
Jaguar Zn Cu
Sinclair
Bentley Zn Fe Cu
King of the Hills
Mt Bevan
Murrin Murrin
Sons of Gw
Leinster
Agnew

ANDRÉ-MARIE AMPÈRE

# ELECTRIC MOTORS AND MAGNETS

In 1820, a French physicist by the name of André-Marie Ampère discovered that there was an amazing connection between electricity and magnetic fields. His discovery made the electric motor possible.

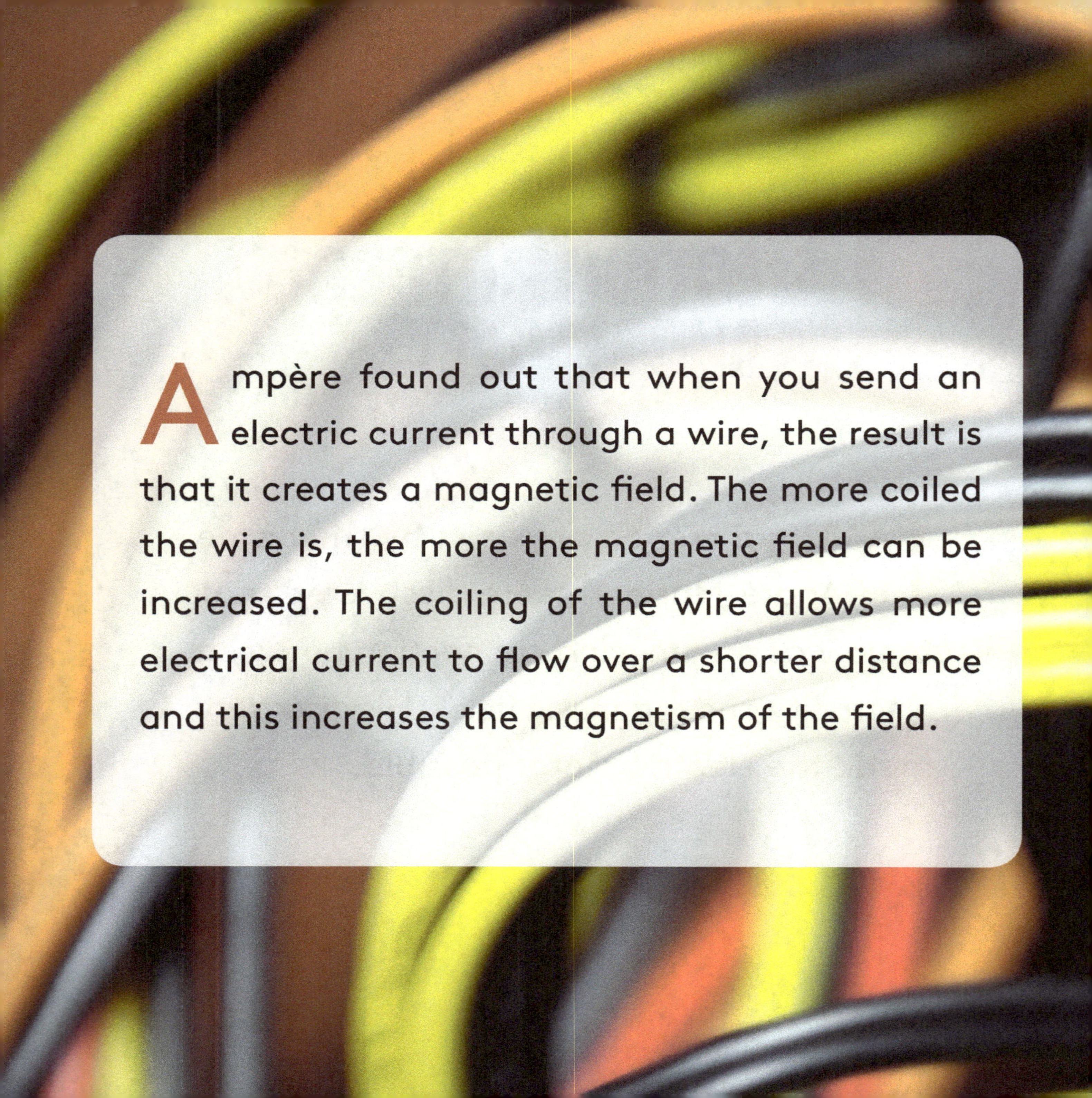

Ampère found out that when you send an electric current through a wire, the result is that it creates a magnetic field. The more coiled the wire is, the more the magnetic field can be increased. The coiling of the wire allows more electrical current to flow over a shorter distance and this increases the magnetism of the field.

ELECTRICAL WIRING

MICHAEL FARADAY

The findings of three inventors had to be added to Ampère's knowledge to create the practical electric motors that we use in our homes today. Those inventors were Michael Faraday, Joseph Henry, and William Sturgeon.

In 1821, Faraday created the very first electrical motor, which used the force of magnetism to work. He took a large nail and wrapped a wire around it about 100 times. Then, he connected the wire to a battery. This gave him an electromagnet that had a north as well as a south pole just like a permanent horseshoe magnet.

MICHAEL FARADAYS 1845 MAGNETO-OPTICAL
ELECTRO-MAGNET & A SECTORED DISC.

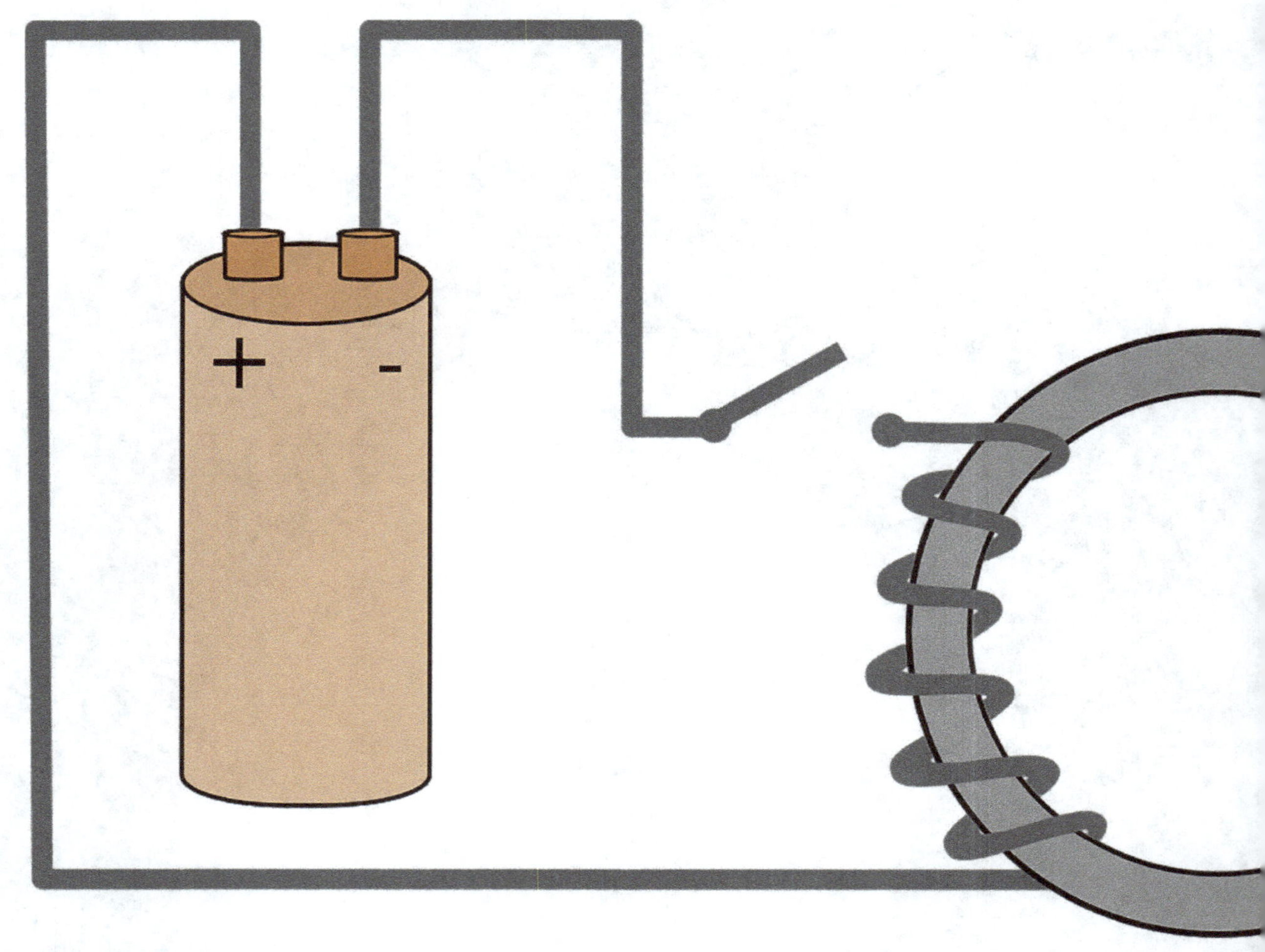


## ELECTROMAGNETIC FIELD EXPERIMENT

Unlike permanent magnets, electromagnets are only temporary and only work when an electrical current is passing through them. That's why he needed

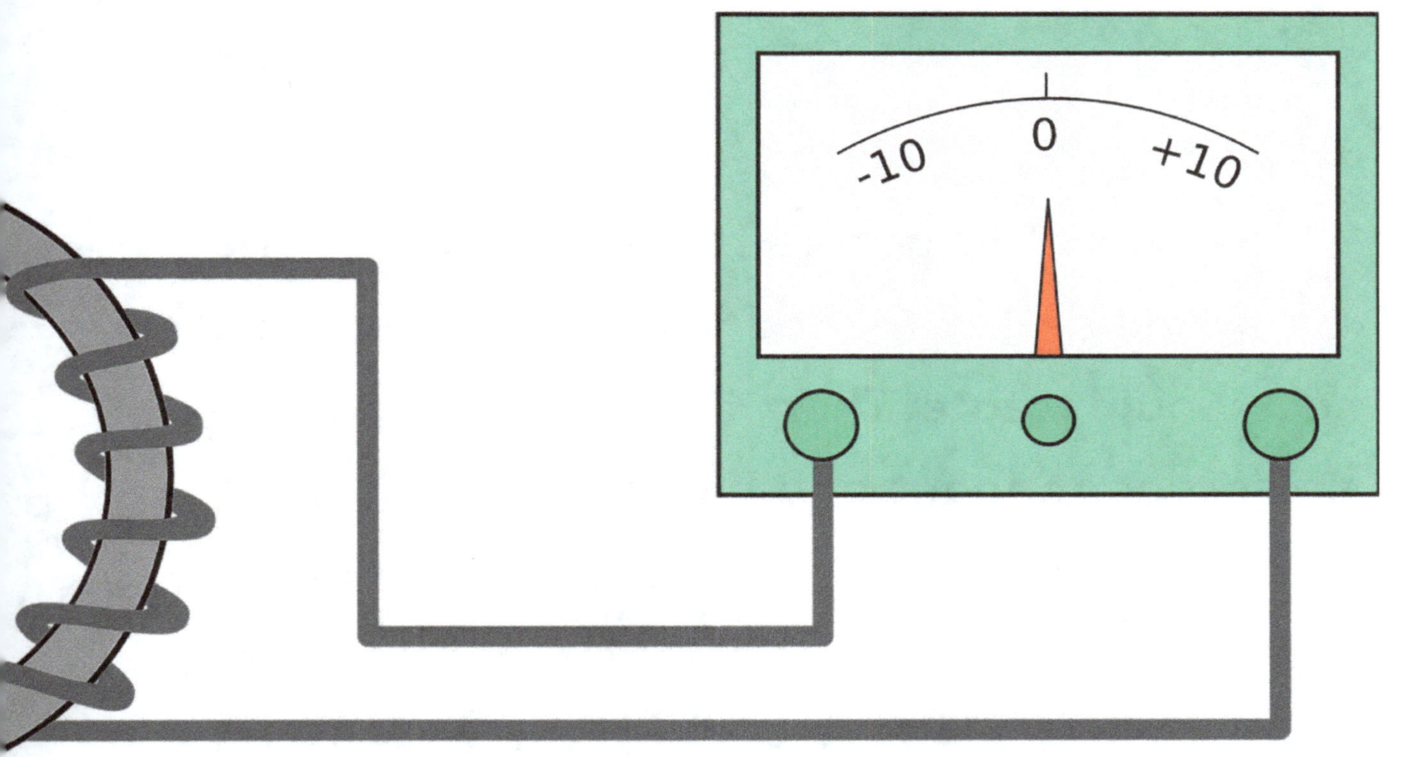

to connect it to a battery to get the current flowing through it. If you reverse the direction of the current, the poles of the electromagnet also reverse.

He created a hole in the middle of the nail and attached the nail to a spindle so it would rotate. Then, he took a permanent horseshoe magnet and placed the nail in the center of the magnet. Next, he connected the wire's north pole to the battery's negative pole. He also connected the wire's south pole to the battery's positive pole.

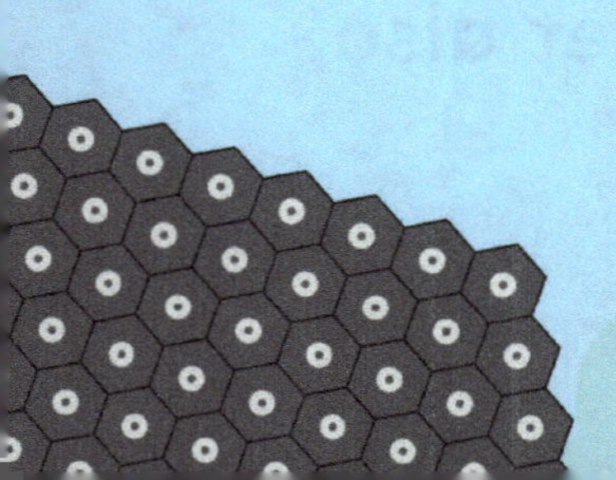

FARADAY'S ELECTROMAGNETIC
INDUCTION EXPERIMENT

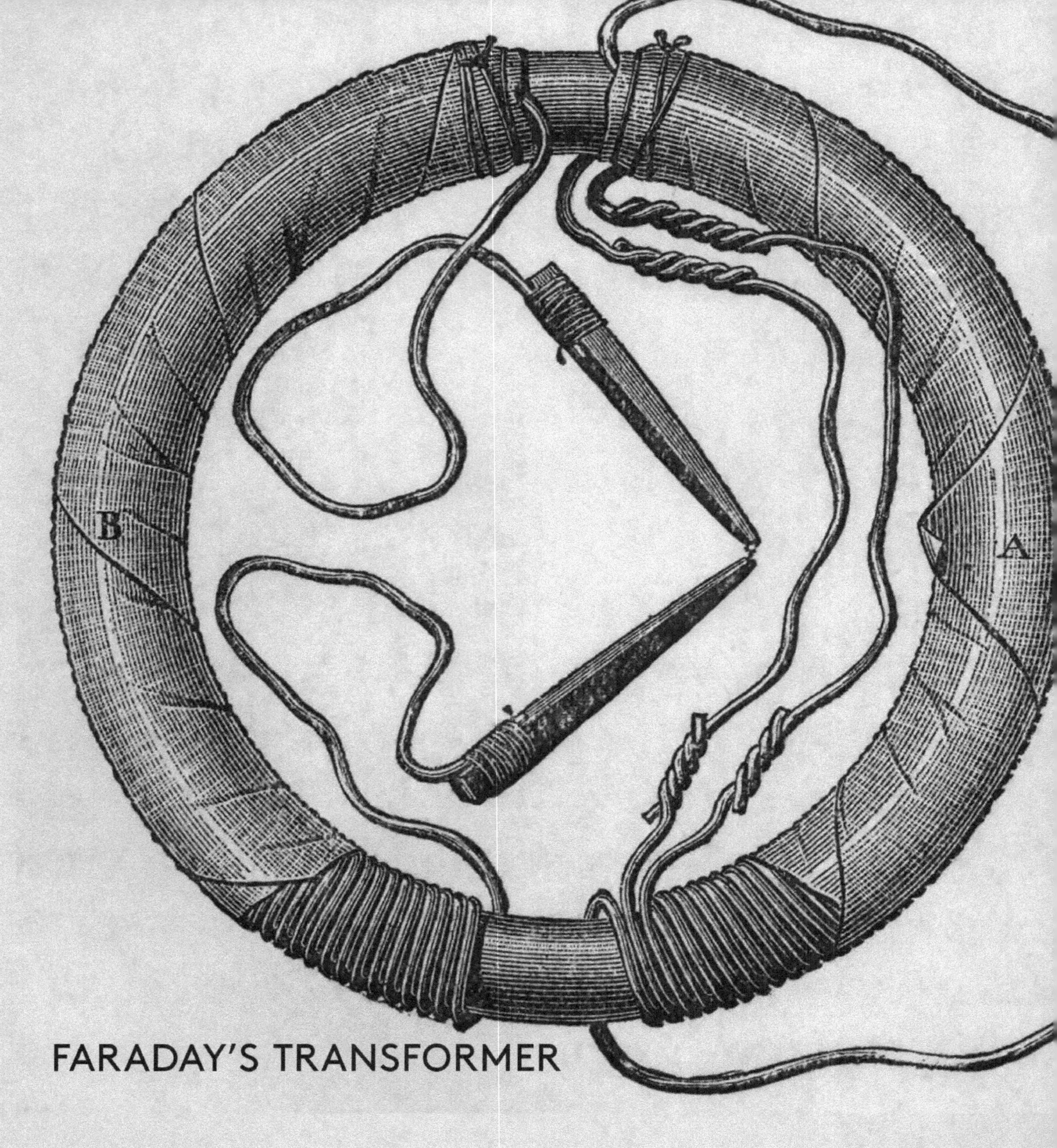


FARADAY'S TRANSFORMER

Now he knew what would happen. The north ends of the electromagnet and the horseshoe magnet would repel each other. The north end of the electromagnet would attract the south pole of the permanent magnet. The attracting force and repelling force would make the nail turn. The motor only turned once but it was enough to see that it would work. Faraday had to continue his work until he could figure out how to get the nail to continue to rotate.

wesome! Now you know more about magnets. You can find more How Things Work books from Baby Professor by searching the website of your favorite book retailer.

Visit
BABY PROFESSOR
EDUCATION KIDS
www.BabyProfessorBooks.com
to download Free Baby Professor eBooks
and view our catalog of new and exciting
Children's Books

www.ingramcontent.com/pod-product-compliance
Lightning Source LLC
Chambersburg PA
CBHW081148180726
48003CB00026B/2936